D-DAY BEACHES
AN ILLUSTRATED COMPANION

D-DAY BEACHES
AN ILLUSTRATED COMPANION

DAVID & CAROL EVANS

AMBERLEY

First published 2012

Amberley Publishing
The Hill, Stroud
Gloucestershire, GL5 4EP

www.amberley-books.com

British Library Cataloguing in Publication Data.
A catalogue record for this book is available from the British Library.

ISBN 978 1 84868 767 7

Typeset in 10pt on 12pt Sabon.
Typesetting and Origination by Amberley Publishing.
Printed in the UK.

CONTENTS

Preface	7
The D-Day Landing Beaches	9
Utah Beach	9
Omaha Beach	9
Gold Beach	11
Juno Beach	13
Sword Beach	13
Amfreville	15
Arromanches-les-Bains	15
The Mulberry Harbours	15
Asnelles-sur-Mer	18
Audrieu	20
Authie	20
Barfleur	23
Basly	23
Bayeux	23
Bazenville	33
Bénouville	36
Bény-sur-Mer	36
Bernières-sur-Mer	40
Bretteville L'Orguelleuse	40
Bréville-les-Monts	44
Brouay	48
Buron	52
Caen	54
Cambes-en-Plaine	57
Carentan	59
Carpiquet	63
Chef-du-Pont	64

Cherbourg	66
Colleville-Montgomery	70
Courseulles-sur-Mer	74
Creully	75
Crisbecq	79
Douvres La Délivrande	80
Escoville	83
Fontenay-Le-Pesnel	83
Grandcamp-Maisy and Pointe Du Hoc	86
Graye-sur-Mer	91
Hermanville-sur-Mer	94
Hill 112 – 'Cornwall Hill'	94
Hottot-les-Bagues	98
Isigny-sur-Mer	100
La Cambe and Orglandes – German War Cemeteries	101
Langrune-sur-Mer	104
Lion-sur-Mer	106
Longues-sur-Mer	108
Luc-sur-Mer	108
Merville-Franceville	111
Montebourg	115
Pegasus Bridge	117
Port-en-Bessin	122
Ranville	124
Ryes	127
St Aubin-sur-Mer	128
St Laurent-sur-Mer and the American Military Cemetery and Memorial	130
Ste Marie du Mont	134
Ste Mère-Église	137
Secqueville-en-Bessin	141
Tilly-sur-Seulles	143
Troarn	145
Valognes	146
Ver-sur-Mer	149
Vierville-sur-Mer	151

PREFACE

War, so says *Chambers English Dictionary*, is a 'state of conflict', 'a long-continued struggle often between impersonal forces' or simply 'a contest between nations carried on by arms'. Over the years, we have travelled the world and visited many different battle sites both at home and abroad – Hastings (1066), Evesham (1265), Bannockburn (1314), Crécy (1346), Agincourt (1415), Tewkesbury (1471), Bosworth (1485), Killiecrankie (1689), the Alamo (1836), Vicksburg (1863), Isandlwana and Ulundi (1879), Ladysmith (1899), Spion Kop (1900), the Gallipoli Campaign (1915), Verdun and the Somme (1916), Passchendaele (1917) ... and, on numerous occasions, the Normandy beaches (1944).

All battles involve courage and determination and result in casualties that include men killed, wounded and missing. While the exact number will never be known, it is estimated that the Normandy invasion cost the United States 29,000 killed and 106,000 wounded and missing. British casualties totalled 11,000 killed and 54,000 wounded and missing, whilst Canadian casualties came to 5,000 killed with 13,000 wounded and missing. In addition, 12,200 French civilians were killed and wounded. Overall, it was a sacrifice of a large number but, put in perspective, it is necessary to remember that on the first day of the Battle of the Somme in 1916 British killed and wounded totalled 60,000 and the battle itself a massive 420,000!

Of course, the Normandy campaign differed from most others. To start with, when recalling events in history, a year is sufficient. D-Day, however, tends to be remembered by the day, month and year. The landings themselves involved crossing the English Channel, landing on beaches that were ready to repel an invasion, and then fighting a way inland when opposed by an enemy holding prepared defensive positions. Since these events occurred only sixty-nine years ago and, therefore, might be considered relatively recent, the beaches and battlefields still hold a special appeal and each year large numbers of veterans, relatives, school parties and tourists return to Normandy and, for many, it has become a place of pilgrimage.

For help in the preparation of this book we are very much indebted to Guy and Nelly Herry, who lived in Normandy during the years of the German occupation and then faced the realities of liberation. More recently they provided us with information and took us on a guided tour of parts of the Contentin Peninsular. Our thanks are also extended to Frank Horrocks who served in the Royal Fusiliers, crossed to Normandy on 7 June 1944 and was involved in the construction of the Mulberry Harbour at Arromanches. He, too, has provided us with much useful information. Finally, Geoffrey Salter's technical advice in preparing the layout of the book and printing the initial manuscript has also been much appreciated.

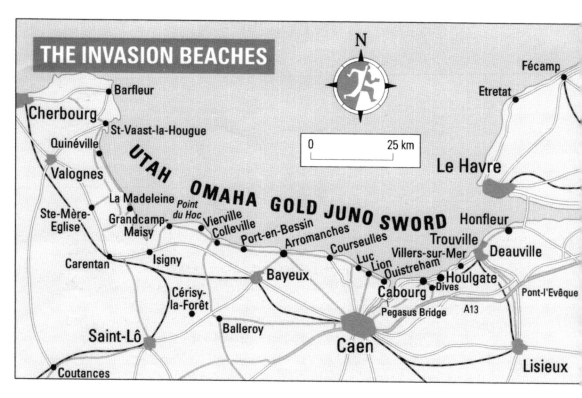

THE D-DAY LANDING BEACHES

Utah Beach

At 6.30 a.m. on 6 June 1944, the first American soldiers to land on Utah Beach were the men of the 1st and 2nd Battalion of the 8th Regimental Combat Team of the US 4th Infantry Division. Along the 5 kilometre beach, they met light opposition and this was because they had inadvertently come ashore 2 kilometres away from the designated landing area and at a place where the German defences were relatively weak. By midday, they were ready to move inland with the aim of linking up with the airborne forces that had landed to the north close to Ste Mère-Église. They intended to cut the main road leading to Carentan and effectively isolate the Contentin Peninsula. Their ultimate aim was to reach the port of Cherbourg in the minimum of time. By the end of D-Day, the US forces had achieved their objectives and 23,000 US troops had landed on Utah Beach. The division losses were extremely light with just 197 men killed and wounded.

Omaha Beach

If the success of the Americans at Utah Beach was achieved with unexpected ease, the same could certainly not be said for the landing on Omaha beach. Some 18 kilometres from the coast, the men intended to be first on the beach boarded their landing craft and, because of the heavy seas, a number of the landing craft and amphibious tanks were swamped and many of the men drowned. The men that made it ashore came from a company of the 116th Infantry Regiment and the 29th Division (National Guard) and found that, ahead of them, the German defenders had the advantage of positions on high ground and were able to rake the beach ahead of them with withering rifle and machine-gun fire. The Americans, stranded at the water's edge, did what they could to move ahead to find shelter and an exit from the beach but the area became a scene of

American forces landing on Utah Beach.

US soldiers struggle ashore on Omaha Beach.

utter chaos with the beach littered with the debris of shattered landing craft and the bodies of the dead and wounded. At one stage, the position became so critical that the American commander, General Omar Bradley, seriously considered withdrawing American forces. Aware of the situation, British and American destroyers came close to the shore to engage German positions and this eased the situation. By 7.30 a.m., the position had started to improve and, within two hours, the Americans had managed to create an exit from the beach and reach the high ground ahead and advance inland to overrun the German positions. The turmoil of the day led to the Americans suffering over 2,000 casualties.

Gold Beach

After a two-hour naval bombardment, at 7.25 a.m. on D-Day the 50th British (Northumbrian) Infantry Division went ashore on Gold Beach, a 5 kilometre stretch of the coast that lay between Ver-sur-Mer and Asnelles. Their mission was to capture the high ground overlooking Arromanches in order to safeguard the planned artificial harbour from German artillery fire and then to advance inland towards Bayeux. Men of the 6th Green Howards, the 1st Hampshire Regiment supported by the tanks of the Westminster Dragoons quickly overcame the German strong points before advancing further inland to silence the German gun batteries. By the evening of 6 June almost all of the 50th Infantry Division's objectives had been achieved. During the course of the day, 25,000 British troops had landed on Gold Beach of which 413 had been killed or wounded.

One of the more unusual British memorials on Gold Beach.

The Canadian 3rd Infantry landing on Juno Beach.

The memorial dedicated to Commandant Kieffer's French Commandos that landed on Sword Beach on D-Day.

Juno Beach

Juno, a 7 kilometre stretch of beach between Graye-sur-Maer and St Aubin-sur-Mer, was the landing area allocated to the 3rd Canadian Infantry Division under Major-General R. F. L. Keller. The main objective for the Canadians was to capture Carpiquet airfield to the west of Caen and also link up with the British who had landed on Gold and Sword beaches. Once the beach had been cleared, the Canadians advanced inland to liberate the villages of Graye-sur-Mer, Courselles and Bernières. To the west, the Canadians quickly linked up with the British on Gold Beach but joining up with those from Sword Beach was much more difficult because of counter-attacks launched by the 192nd German Panzer Grenadier Regiment. Of the 15,000 men involved in the landing 946 were killed or wounded.

Sword Beach

Sword Beach was the eastern end of the planned invasion area and was allocated to the British 3rd Infantry Division led by Major-General T. G. Rennie. The beach extended just 2 kilometres from Lion-sur-Mer to Ouistreham and the first ashore were the 1st South Lancashire and 2nd East Yorkshire Regiments supported by tanks of the 13th/18th Hussars. The main objectives were to first establish a bridgehead and then advance on the city of Caen. It was here that Lord Lovat's 1st Special Service Brigade and the Commandent Kieffer's French Commandos were involved. Lovat's men were intended to link up with the 8th Airborne paratroopers and reinforce the bridgehead on the east side of the River Orne whilst Keiffer's French Commandos were expected to advance to Rivan Bella and then reach Ouistreham. Whilst the 3rd Infantry Division failed to capture all its objectives again because of the fierce counter-attacks by the German 192 Panzer Grenadier Regiment, the following morning they did link up with the Canadians advancing along the coast from Juno beach. At the end of the day, the 3rd British Infantry Division had landed 28,845 soldiers on Sword Beach with the loss of 630 men killed or wounded.

Amfreville

Amfreville lies on the eastern bank of the River Orne and on the morning of D-Day, it was one of the first villages to be liberated by men of the No. 6 Commando. Later it became the scene of heavy fighting when it was used to protect the British positions on the eastern flank of Sword Beach by neutralising a German battery and winning control of several bridges. During the afternoon, the British position was reinforced by Lord Lovat's 1st Special Brigade and, later, by the arrival of French No. 3 Commando led by Commander Phillipe Kieffer. Today, close to the church are memorials to No. 6 Commando, the First Special Service Brigade and to the British and French Commandos who reached the area on the first morning of D-Day. The village green, *Le Plain Place de Commandant Kieffer*, is dedicated to the leader of the French Commandos.

Arromanches-les-Bains

A popular pre-war seaside resort, on D-Day Arromanches-les-Bains lay on the edge of Gold Beach. The first British tanks entered the town during the afternoon of 6 June but, due to strong German resistance, it was not liberated until following day. Without any major ports at the disposal of the Allies, it was essential that work began on the construction of an artificial harbour, a Mulberry harbour later to be known as Port Winston. Today Arromanches is again a bustling seaside resort. With many souvenir shops and an impressive museum it attracts veterans and tourists visiting the region of the D-Day landings.

The Mulberry Harbours

Until such time as major ports such as Cherbourg and Le Havre could be used by the Allies, plans were made to construct prefabricated harbours out of blocks of concrete

Local townsfolk make friends
with Frenchmen serving
with No. 10 Commandos at
Amfreville in June 1944.

Close to St Martin's church
are memorials to soldiers
who lost their lives liberating
the town.

The town's impressive D-Day museum.

The town celebrates the 65th anniversary of D-Day.

Parts of the Mulberry harbours have survived and can be reached at low tide.

Army vehicles coming ashore from the Mulberry Harbour at Arromanches.

that were to be made in Britain and then towed across the English Channel by tugs. Known as Mulberry harbours, one was erected at Arromanches and the other at Saint Laurent-sur-Mer close to the American landing site at Omaha Beach. The British Mulberry survived and was extensively used for six months but the American Mulberry lasted only a fortnight before it was destroyed by a storm.

Asnelles-sur-Mer

The small coastal resort of Asnelles-sur-Mer lies between Arromanches-les-Bains and Ver-sur-Mer. As a part of Gold Beach, on D-Day the British forces were led ashore by men of the 231st Infantry Brigade of the 50th Northumbrian Division which included the First Battalions of the Dorset, Devonshire and Hampshire regiments. They immediately came under heavy German fire and it took some time before they could move off the beach and advance on the town. They suffered some two hundred casualties but managed to liberate the area the next day. Today, the crossroads in the centre of the village is named after the commander of the 231st Infantry Brigade, Place Alexander Stanier, and nearby there is a Rue de Southampton and a Rue The Devonshire Regiment. There is also an unusual wall-like monument dedicated to the 50th Northumbrian Division.

A memorial in Devon Regiment Road dedicated to the 231st Infantry Brigade.

From the remains of an old German bunker it is possible to enjoy a panoramic view of Asnelles.

Audrieu

The village of Audrieu lies to the north-west of Caen. On 8 June 1944, the positions held by the Canadian Royal Winnipeg Rifles were overrun by the German 12th SS Panzers which was part of the Hitler Jugend (Hitler Youth) Division. There were heavy losses on both sides and afterwards, on 8, 9 and 11 June, the fanatical German teenagers commanded by Colonel Kurt Meyer went on an orgy of murdering the Canadian prisoners-of-war they had captured. The atrocities were committed in the grounds of Le Château d'Audrieu. After the war, Meyer faced numerous charges of murdering Allied prisoners-of-war. Found guilty and sentenced to death, his sentence was later commuted to life imprisonment. He was released in 1954.

Born in 1910, the son of a factory worker, he became an officer in the Waffen-SS and was rapidly promoted to become the youngest divisional commander in the German Army. Even before D-Day, he had a reputation for committing outrages on the Eastern Front. After the war, he was put on trial and accused of five criminal offences, found guilty, was sentenced to death. After release, Meyer worked for a German brewery until he died in December 1961 on his fifty-first birthday.

Authie

Authie, which lies 2 kilometres to the north-west of Caen, was liberated by the Canadian North Nova Scotia Highlanders on 7 June but was then almost immediately re-taken by the tanks of Kurt Meyer's 12th SS Panzer Division. On 8 July, the Canadians again advanced on Authie and the village was finally taken but at the cost of a 160 casualties

The Château d'Audrieu in the grounds of which the atrocities against Canadian prisoners-of-war were committed.

Colonel Kurt Meyer.

Canadian soldiers searching German prisoners-of-war.

Soldiers making a scarecrow
out of a German SS uniform.

and the loss of 7 Sherman tanks. Afterwards the front stabilised and plans were made to advance on the city of Caen.

Barfleur

Twenty kilometres to the east of Cherbourg, Barfleur is a fishing harbour situated on the corner of the Contentin Peninsular. The port is famous for the events that occurred during its long and distinguished history, many of which involved England. In 1066, it was the port from which William of Normandy (now better known as William the Conqueror) set sail for England to defeat Harold in a battle fought at Senlac Hill close to Hastings. In 1120, a vessel, known as the *White Ship*, on its way from Normandy to England struck rocks off the Pointe de Barfleur and sank. Amongst those who drowned was William, the only legitimate son of Henry I and heir to the English throne. The sinking of the ship was attributed to the fact that many of the crew were drunk. His death led to a disputed succession to the English throne between Stephen and Matilda and this was followed by years of anarchy. In 1692, a combined fleet of British and Dutch ships fought a sea battle off the Pointe de Barfleur against a French fleet under Admiral de Tourville. Known as the Battle of La Hogue, both sides suffered heavy losses but eventually the French fleet was dispersed.

Barfleur contributed little to the events of D-Day. Even so, the people of the town must have been well aware of what was happening 60 kilometres to the south at Utah Beach and Ste Mère-Église. Although the port had been fortified by the Germans, the town was not defended and was taken by the Americans on 21 June 1944 without a struggle.

Basly

Basly is a village close to Bény-sur-Mer that was liberated by the Régiment de la Chaudière of the Canadian 3rd Infantry Division on D-Day.

Bayeux

Long famous for its cathedral and tapestry, Bayeux lies due south from Gold Beach and its capture was a major Allied objective of D-Day. Although the British 50th Division reached the outskirts of the town by the evening of 6 June, they hesitated to occupy the town as darkness fell and waited until the following morning. After four years of occupation, on 7 June 1944, the Germans left Bayeux undefended and the city became one of the first sizeable French towns to be liberated. A week later, General Charles de Gaulle, leader of the Free French movement, entered the town in triumph and made a celebrated speech in a local park – now the Place Charles de Gaulle.

The city's famous Bayeux tapestry is 70 metres long and relates to the events leading to the Battle of Hastings and the subsequent Norman conquest of England. It is made

A memorial in Authie dedicated to men of the North Nova Scotia Highlanders who fought to liberate their village.

A painting illustrating the fate of the *White Ship*.

A painting by Benjamin West (1738–1820) depicting the Battle of La Hogue.

One of the numerous German bunkers around Barfleur that were unused on D-Day or afterwards.

Barfleur today. Dominated by the impressive Church of St Nicholas, the town remains a very active fishing port.

up of linen embroidered with a range of coloured yarns and has Latin captions. During the war, the tapestry was moved to the Louvre in Paris and, after the liberation of the city, returned to be lodged in Bayeux cathedral. Today it can be seen in the *Centre Guillaume le Conqueerant* in the city.

The city's cathedral dates from 1077 and amongst its many memorials is one to the memory of 'one million dead of the British Empire who fell in the Great War', another to the 56th British Infantry Brigade who 'died in the campaign for the liberation of North Western Europe – June 1944 – May 1945' and yet another to the 50th Northumbrian Division 'who laid down their lives for justice, freedom and the liberation of France...' There is also a stained glass window dedicated to men of the Allied sea, land and air forces who took part in the D-Day and Normandy operations. Close to the cathedral is a memorial to local French people who were deported and died in Nazi concentration camps.

The truly impressive British War Cemetery is the largest military cemetery of the Second World War to be found in France. It contains 4,648 graves that include 3,935 British, 466 German, 25 Polish and smaller numbers from other countries involved in the conflict. Directly opposite is the Bayeux War Memorial. Designed by Philip Hepworth, it has engraved on it the names of 1,808 men of Britain and the Commonwealth that died in the battle for Normandy but who have no known grave. The Latin inscription: *Nos a Guliemo Victi Victoris Patrium Liberavimus* – We, once conquered by William have now set free the Conqueror's native land. Another group of British soldiers of the Rifle Brigade is buried in the city's Cimetiere Saint Exupere.

Basly today. A maple-leaf shaped memorial with the inscription 'Recollection and gratitude to the Canadian liberators. The 6 June 1944.'

Soldiers of the Royal Canadian Army Medical Corps placing flowers on the graves of fallen comrades.

A section of the Bayeux tapestry.

General de Gaulle on his arrival in Bayeux in June 1944.

Bayeux cathedral.

The memorial to local people who were deported or died in Nazi concentration camps.

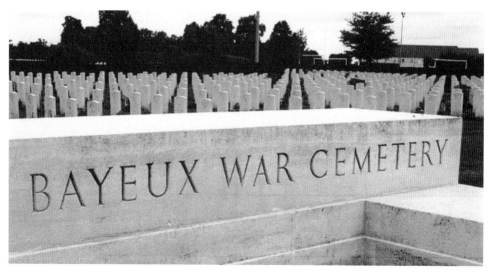

Bayeux War Cemetery.

The Bayeux War Memorial.

A typical street scene in Bayeux as it is today.

An impressive Battle of Normandy Memorial Museum was specially designed to house an exhibition of weapons, transport and other memorabilia of D-Day and is situated opposite the war cemetery.

Bazenville

One of the essential needs after the invasion of Normandy was to establish airfields capable of providing cover for the invading troops and these had to be quickly constructed and made operational. Amongst these was one built at Bazenville, 12 kilometres to the north-east of Bayeux. Whilst the village itself played little part in the events of D-Day, the hastily built airfield soon gave it considerable importance.

The airfield was built by the Royal Engineers 16th Airfield Construction Group with the assistance of others and was completed just after midnight on D-Day. The airfield consisted of a runway, dispersal areas, landing lights and all the facilities needed to run an airfield. The hangars and other buildings largely consisted of canvas-type materials. During a period from mid-June to mid-August 1944, the airfield was used by 403, 416 and 421 Squadrons of the Royal Canadian Air Force.

The land occupied by the Bazenville airfield was returned to local farmers. Today, visitors to the area find it difficult to locate the runway in what is now a series of ploughed fields surrounded by scrub and brush. Even so, it is occasionally possible to discover pieces of tubing and metal. In front of the local church are memorials, one of them in the shape of a Spitfire wing.

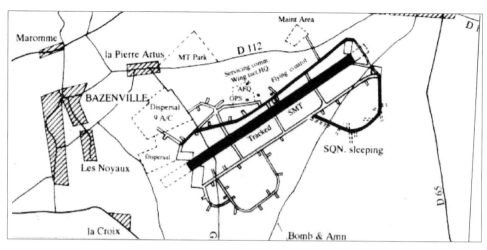

A diagram of the airfield.

An aerial view of the completed airfield.

Members of 174 Squadron playing cricket against the background of a Hawker Typhoon being serviced outside a hangar.

Hawker Typhoon pilots of 181 Squadron leave after a briefing to take part in a sortie over Normandy.

A memorial in the shape of a Spitfire wing.

Bénouville

Bénouville lies on the west bank of the River Orne and close to the famous Pegasus Bridge (see pages 117). The first troops to land in the area arrived in six gliders carrying men of the 2nd Battalion of the Oxfordshire and Buckinghamshire Light Infantry under the command of Major John Howard. Shortly after midnight they were followed by paratroopers of the 7th Light Infantry Battalion of the Parachute Regiment. Hours later, the 7th Parachute Battalion crossed the canal bridge and took up position in Bénouville and held their positions through a difficult day of continuous German shelling. That evening troops that had landed on Sword Beach arrived and the next morning they fought their way inland.

Today, a plaque on the *mairie* claims that it was the first French town hall to be liberated on D-Day when British paratroopers landed there just before midnight on 5 June. Opposite is a memorial crucifix dedicated to the 7th Light Infantry Battalion of the Parachute Regiment. The road leading on towards Pegasus Bridge was later named *Avenue du Commandant Keiffer*, after the leader of the French Commandos. In Bénouville there is all so an eighteenth-century château which, during the years of German occupation, was run by Madame Vion as a home for unmarried mothers. Madame Vion strongly resisted German attempts to take over her home. Bénouville churchyard contains the graves of twenty-two British soldiers the majority of which belonged to the 6th Airborne Division. They include the grave of the Reverend George Parry, an army chaplain from Leytonstone in Essex who was killed on D-Day.

Bény-sur-Mer

The Régiment de la Chaudière of the Canadian 3rd Infantry Division was a French-Canadian regiment from the province of Quebec. Their task, after landing near Bernières on the morning of D-Day (see page 40) was to advance south until they came into contact with the Germans and this they did at Bény-sur-Mer. In spite of tough German resistance, they managed to liberate the village late in the afternoon.

Later, Bény-sur-Mer became the site of a Canadian war cemetery with a total of 2,049 graves that included nine sets of brothers. These included Gordon and Ronald Branton from Lethbridge, Alberta. Buried close together, their inscription reads: 'We left with a jest our home in the west. Now with the best we lie at rest.' Another grave is that of R. Guenard, a French resistance fighter who chose to fight alongside the Canadian troops during the Normandy campaign. Having no known relatives, he was placed among the soldiers whose conflict he shared. The plaque on his cross reads simply: '*Mort pour la France, 19.7.1944.*'

A German sniper using the church caused problems and had to be dealt with by using a shell to blow a hole in the tower.

Bénouville today. The church with its tower restored.

Canadian troops entering Bény-sur-Mer on D-Day.

Local children placing flowers on the memorial in the cemetery in 1969.

The splendid Château de Bénouville as it appears today.

Bény-sur-Mer today. A war memorial to the Régiment de la Chaudière can be seen in front of the church.

Bernières-sur-Mer

On 6 June 1944, the Canadian 8th Infantry Brigade, part of the Canadian 3rd Infantry Division, was allocated a landing area on Juno Beach, known as NAN White, opposite the town of Bernières-sur-Mer. It was a difficult task since the German beach obstacles were virtually intact and the soldiers landing faced concrete bunkers and murderous small-arms fire from machine-gun positions ahead of them. They had no choice but to make a dash across the beach to seek shelter at the foot of the promenade wall. Fortunately, some amphibious tanks launched a short distance offshore were soon able to support the infantry. During the course of the day, showing exemplary courage, the Canadians managed to overcome the enemy positions along the waterfront but the number of casualties suffered by the Queen's Own Rifles was close to half their number and exceeded that of any other Canadian unit. However, thanks to the courage of a ship's officer who brought his craft close inshore and used anti-aircraft shells to eliminate a German strong point whilst a bulldozer was used to silence a pillbox by filling it with sand. Afterwards, the Canadians were able to fight their way inland towards Bény-sur-Mer until German resistance again became so intense that they were forced to halt. Back on the beach, men and equipment continued to come ashore and this led to a pile up.

Today, the area has numerous memorials that recognise the bravery of the Canadians on D-Day. On the promenade in a place known as the Place du Canada there is a Comite du Debarquement Memorial next to an armoured car of the Queens Own Rifles as well as a memorial to the Régiment de la Chaudière.

Bretteville L'Orguelleuse

Bretteville L'Orguelleuse lies 16 kilometres to the east of Bayeux. On the evening of D-Day, units of the Canadian Regina Rifle Regiment reached the village as they edged their way towards Caen. The next morning, the 12th SS Panzer-Division launched a fierce counter-attack, succeeded in getting dangerously close to the Canadian headquarters and forced them to withdraw. On 9 June, the Royal Winnipeg Rifles counter-attacked and on 9 June forced the Germans to pull back and were finally able to liberate the town. The liberation of Bretteville L'Orguelleuse proved an expensive operation with the Canadians suffering nearly four hundred casualties.

Today there is an elegant memorial in the village square dedicated to the Regina Rifle Regiment. It is inscribed '*Noublie pas Juin 1944*'. Close by is another memorial which lists the people of Bretteville L'Orguelleuse who lost their lives during the Second World War: '*Aux enfants de Bretteville morts pour la France*'. The memorial also gives details of the part played by members of the Lecanu family in the war (see pages 51–52).

Canadian soldiers coming ashore at Bernières-sur-Mer with their bicycles.

German prisoners-of-war with their Canadian guards close to the beach at Bernières-sur-Mer.

A German bunker turned into a memorial at Bernières-sur-Mer.

A memorial to the Régiment de la Chaudière close to the beach at Bernières-sur-Mer.

A splendid Norman house at Bernières-sur-Mer in war and peace. As the house appeared after D-Day in 1944.

The extent of the destruction in the village of Bretteville L'Orguelleuse during June 1944.

A mortar crew of the Regina Rifle Regiment in action near the village.

Bréville-les-Monts

Bréville-les-Monts lies on high ground with the outskirts of Caen clearly visible in the distance and, because of its strategic importance, the Germans were determined to vigorously defend the village. Consequently, during the immediate post D-Day period, it became the scene of extremely ferocious fighting between the British 6th Airborne Division and the German 346th Infantry Division. The capture of the village was first allocated to the 3rd Parachute Brigade that landed near the near the village on the night of 5/6 June but on 10 June the village was still in German hands. As the days passed, it became increasingly clear that the Germans might create a gap in the perimeter of the British line and that the high ground needed to be taken urgently. On 11 June, the paratroopers, now reinforced by the Black Watch, attempted a new assault but again it failed with the Scottish regiment suffering some two hundred casualties.

The following day, the 12th Parachute Regiment, the 12th Devonshires and tanks of the 13th/18th Hussars attacked the German positions and were furiously resisted. To make matters worse, some of the advancing British troops were cut down by their own supporting artillery whose barrage fell short. Again casualties were high for both sides with the Germans losing 418 out of their 564 men. Nevertheless, by the end of the day the British had reached and secured the village.

The nearby Château St Come, known as a famous stud home and for its racing stables, suffered appallingly when, occupied by the Devonshire Regiment, the stables were reduced to rubble and many of the horses killed. The war chronicle of the

German soldiers move forward to defend Bréville-Les-Monts.

British paratroopers after they had taken the village.

Church of Saint-Pierre reduced to ruins during the battle for Bréville-Les-Monts.

The Château St Come as it is today.

Amongst the memorials is one dedicated to the 51st Highland Infantry.

Oxfordshire and Buckingham Light Infantry recalls, 'it was pathetic to see wounded mares and fouls struggling in the fields, and somewhat precarious to go to help them owing to the presence of enemy snipers. The value of the horses destroyed must have been very great.' After the loss of Bréville-les-Monts, the Germans never seriously tried to retake the village or attack the airborne division's lines again.

Today Bréville-les-Monts has been restored and again has the appearance of a typical Norman village. Opposite the church of Saint Pierre is a memorial to the men of the Parachute and Devonshire regiments who had played a major role in liberating the village. In the church cemetery amongst the civilian graves are the headstones of two British soldiers killed on 12 June. Near the Château St Come is a monument dedicated to the 9th Parachute Regiment.

Brouay

Brouay lies just off the main road between Caen and Bayeux and, during the period of 10 and 18 June, it became part of the front line village when British forces entered the village and then edged eastward to begin the encirclement of Caen. The fighting in that region of Normandy led to heavy casualties on both sides and many of those that lost their lives were brought to Brouay for burial in a military cemetery adjacent to the village church. These included men serving in the Corps of Military Police, the East Riding Yeomanry, the King's Own Yorkshire Light Infantry the Oxfordshire and Buckinghamshire Light Infantry, and in one section, known as 'Welsh Corner', men of the South Wales Borderers, the Welch Regiment and the Monmouthshire Regiment.

Amongst those buried in the cemetery are Lt Col. Edward Ripley who commanded the 1/5th Battalion of the Welch Regiment and the chaplain Reverend Harry Smith

Brouay Military Cemetery today.

The graves of the seven military policemen in Brouay War Cemetery: L/Cpl Philip Benjafield, L/Cpl John Churchyard, L/Cpl Frederick Greenstreet, L/Cpl John Harris, L/Cpl Ronald Hawkins, L/Cpl Jack Hazzard, L/Cpl Norman Penson.

Brouay church.

The grave of the Lecanu family in Brouay churchyard.

A picture of Raymond Lecanu that appears on the grave.

from Littleover, Derby. There are also the graves of seven lance corporals of the Corps of Military Police who were killed on 21 July when a prisoner-of-war cage they were guarding was hit by a German bomb. Of the 377 interred in the Brouay Cemetery all but two Canadians are British.

Amongst the family graves in the churchyard cemetery is a memorial to nineteen-year-old Raymond Lecanu. He was one of the three sons of a baker from Bretteville L'Orguelleuse who all played an active part in the war. Roger, the eldest, crossed to Britain to join the Free French and on D-Day was serving on a minesweeper off the Normandy coast. Louis, like many Frenchmen threatened with deportation to do forced labour in Germany, left the area and instead joined the Maquis to become part of the French Resistance. The youngest brother, Raymond, was left at home but then also joined the Resistance until he was arrested by the Gestapo. Detained in turn in Caen, Paris and Compiègne, he was tortured before being sent to Stutthof concentration camp and then to Dauchau where he died on 9 September 1944. As his brother Louis later said, he was '*palmi celle des autres comrades morts pour la liberte*' – 'he was among other comrades who died for freedom'.

Buron

It was on 7 June that the Canadian 9th Brigade, led by the North Nova Scotia Highlanders and the Sherbrooke Fusiliers of the 27th Armoured Regiment, first moved towards Buron. When still to the north of the village, they came under heavy fire from German machine guns and anti-tank weapons and it was not until midday that they were able to enter Buron. Later, the Germans launched a counter-attack and during the struggle that followed the Highlanders suffered 250 casualties and the Sherbrooks lost 21 tanks. There were also reports that Canadian prisoners had been shot by fanatical young Germans of the 12th SS (Hitler Jugend) Panzer Division commanded by Kurt Meyer (see also pages 20–21). Early the next morning the Canadians again advanced on Buron and once more faced determined opposition and hand-to-hand fighting led to what proved to be yet another costly encounter. During a day long battle fought largely in an open field, the Canadians lost half their men. Later one of those who took part wrote: 'That day, he learned to plant rifles in the ground to mark the dead. He learned what a man looks like after he has been cut to pieces ... He learned you can save a man by using your bare hands to squeeze his brain back into his shattered skull, then bandage it up as tightly as you can.' Little wonder the carnage earned the village the nickname 'Bloody Buron'. On 8 June, German resistance came to an end and the village was finally taken.

The events of that time led to two memorials being erected in the village. In the main square, the Place de Canadiens, there is a memorial to the Highland Infantry of Canada and another to the Sherbrooke Fusiliers.

A Canadian tank of the Sherbrooke Fusiliers abandoned at Buron on 8 July.

Two German prisoners-of-war, one wounded, being escorted by a Canadian soldier.

Caen

Caen, the largest city in Normandy, lies on the River Orne and is the capital of Lower Normandy and the prefecture of Calvados. Originally the home of William the Conqueror (sometimes referred to as William the Bastard) and his wife, Matilda of Flanders, it has an impressive history dating back to the eleventh century and the city grew to become an important port as well as a major industrial, commercial and cultural centre. Its main attractions include a magnificent château begun by William the Conqueror, the *Abbaye-aux-Hommes* dedicated to St Stephen, the *Eglise de la Trinite* (the Church of the Holy Trinity) and the Abbaye aux Dames (the Abbey for Women). The flourishing city centre included a range of splendid houses and impressive architecture. Although some 12 kilometres from the coast, Caen was able to serve as a port due to the River Orne and today due to a canal that stretches inland from Ouistreham. The University of Caen dates from the fifteenth century and was totally destroyed by aerial bombing on 7 July 1944.

The capture of Caen had been a major objective on D-Day but this proved to be impossible. The Allied armies advancing inland were beaten off by German counterattacks and it took two months of bitter fighting before the city finally fell. On 26 June, British troops began Operation *Epsom* with an advance against Caen from the west but

A portrait of William the Conqueror.

found going difficult and the offensive ground to a halt. The consequent war of attrition proved extremely costly to both sides. In order to break the stalemate a final assault was planned, Operation *Charnwood*. On 7 July, as a prelude to the new offensive, British Halifax and Lancaster bombers carried out a thousand bomber raid on the city that raised three-quarters of the centre of Caen to the ground. Unfortunately, the bombing was largely off target and did only limited damage to the German positions.

The next day British groups fought their way into the city where they faced fanatical opposition from the Hitler Jugend, which was part of the 12th SS Panzer Division. Savage house-to-house fighting followed before the west bank of the River Orne was in Allied hands. It took another ten days for an advance to be made on the east bank of the river and the city was not completely liberated until 20 July. During this time, the people of Caen were forced to find shelter wherever they could. Many sought refuge in the city's cathedrals and churches, the hospice of *Bon Sauveur* and the quarries of Fleury but even so some three thousand fell victims of the battle.

In spite of the destruction inflicted on Caen, after the war it gradually emerged from its ruins to once again become an important and historical French city. Today it has

Caen after being bombed on 7 July 1944.

Canadian soldiers make their way through the devastated city.

A memorial at the museum dedicated to peace.

The *Memorial – Un Musée Pour La Paix*.

a great many memorials and monuments dedicated to those who fought to liberate the city. In *Boulevard Bertrand* there is a plaque to the first Canadian soldier to be killed within the city, in the *Place de la Resistance* there is a monument to French men deported by the Germans during the war; in the Rue de la Deliverande is a memorial to all those who lost their lives during the liberation of the city. Within the walls of the château, there are plaques that honour the men who served in the Canadian armed forces and to General de Gaulle, *Liberateur de la France*. At the foot of the steps leading to the battlements is a memorial to the soldiers of the 3rd British Infantry Division. Just off the ring-road, the N13, lies the impressive museum, *Memorial – Un Musée Pour La Paix*. Opened by President Mitterrand on 6 June 1984, it is without doubt one of the most imposing museums dedicated to the Second World War that can be found anywhere and it merits a half day stop rather than a passing visit. Outside there is a *Vallee du Memorial* that includes a monument dedicated to the Frenchmen shot by the Germans whilst held in Caen prison.

Cambes-en-Plaine

Cambes-en-Plaine lies 7 kilometres to the north-west of Caen and by 5 July it had become part of the front line of the 3rd British Infantry Division advancing towards the city. Faced by strong enemy counter-attacks, the fighting was ferocious and the casualties heavy. Amongst the units involved were the 2nd Royal Ulster Rifles, the 6th North Staffords and the 2/6th South Staffords. Cambes-en-Plaine was finally liberated when Operation Charnwood was launched on 8 July.

The entrance to the Cambes-en-Plaine War Cemetery.

The cemetery with its 224 British graves.

Nearby is the impressive Cambes-en-Plaine War Cemetery that contains the graves of 224 British soldiers. With some justification, the cemetery might be rightly called the 'Staffordshire Cemetery' since more than half the burials are of men of the North and South Staffordshire Regiments. Amongst those buried in the cemetery is Regimental Sergeant-Major Robert Hazlehurst of the North Staffords who came from Shrewsbury; another grave is that of nineteen-year-old Private Reginald Parker who served with the 7th Battalion of the South Staffords and was the son of Albert and Edith Parker from Kendal in Westmorland. His parents added to his headstone the poignant comment – 'Goodbye, Reggie, some day maybe we'll understand'.

Carentan

Because Carentan lay in a key position at the neck of the Contentin Peninsula, its speedy capture was of strategic importance to the Allies since it was on the main road that led north to Cherbourg and was at a point where the Peninsula was only 50 kilometres wide. In addition, it would be essentially placed to connect the US 101st Airborne Division advancing south from Ste Mère-Église with US 29th Division moving inland from Omaha Beach. The intention was that, once the town was captured and reinforcements had arrived, the Americans would advance westward and cut off the Contentin Peninsula. However, the capture of Carentan was to prove difficult since the approach to the town passed through waterlogged fields close to the Rivers Douve and Merderet and the German 6th Parachute Regiment was situated where it might offer stubborn resistance and so prevent the American advance.

A French mother looks anxiously as American soldiers treat her wounded child.

American soldiers enter Carentan in a captured German Kübelwagen (bucket seat car).

American soldiers standing before a memorial dedicated to French soldiers who died in the First World War.

The memorial as it appears today.

A Liberation Monument
that recalls the taking of
the town by the American
101st Airborne Division.

After the Americans entered the town on 11 June they faced fierce counter-attacks
by the German 17th Panzer Grenadier Division. At first it seemed that the Germans
might be successful in their defence of the town but the timely arrival of the US 2nd
Armoured Division saved the day for the Americans. Nevertheless, it took two more
days of bitter fighting before Carentan was finally liberated on 12 June.

Although Carentan was severely damaged during the struggle for the town, today
there is little sign of those events though some of the older buildings, such as the church
of *Notre Dame*, still display evidence shell damage. The memorial in the centre of the
town to the fallen of the First World War now includes a panel dedicated '*aux victimes
de la guerre 1939-1945*'.

Outside the town hall there is a *Comité du Débarquement* monument that
commemorates the town's liberation and, at the base, a plaque to honour the Americans
of 101st Airborne Division, the 'Screaming Eagles', who lost their lives during the
Second World War.

Carpiquet

From the start, one of the objectives of 6 June was to capture Carpiquet airfield that served the city of Caen. By the evening of that day, units of the North Nova Scotia Highlanders and the Sherbrook Fusiliers had already reached the outskirts of the town. If they had managed to advance further, the epic battle for Caen might have followed a very different course (see pages 54–57). The small town of Carpiquet was defended by men of the 12th SS Panzer Division who strongly resisted the Canadian advance for a month. On the morning of 8 July, a combined British and Canadian assault in the direction of Caen was launched backed by an artillery bombardment and this led to the liberation of Carpiquet. Afterwards the troops moved forward towards the airfield where, at first, they failed to break through the solid German defences. During the night, the British and Canadians managed to repulse several German attacks on their positions but it was to take three more days of ferocious fighting before they were able to take the airfield.

Today, two memorials exist in the town. One is inscribed '*En souvenir du 4th Jullet 1944. Hommage de la commune de Carpiquet a ses Liberateurs Canadiens*' and the other is dedicated to the officers and men of the North Shore New Brunswick Regiment and the people of Normandy who lost their lives during the Second World War.

A Canadian soldier guards a German taken prisoner at the airport.

The memorial to the North Shore New Brunswick Regiment in the town centre.

Chef-du-Pont

Chef-du-Pont is a small village to the south-east of Ste Mère-Église. On the morning of D-Day, it was the centre of a zone allocated to the 508th Parachute Regiment of the 82nd US Airborne Division. The Americans found that the village was defended by the German 91st Division and, to make matters worse, many of the men landed in flooded fields close to the River Merderet. Weighed down by their heavy equipment, some of the paratroopers drowned. During this time, Maurice Duboscq, a French railwayman, became a hero when he used his boat to rescue American paratroopers struggling in the water. Meanwhile American paratroopers pressed ahead, took control of the bridge over the River Merderet and then drove the Germans from Chef-du-Pont. There German artillery inflicted heavy losses on the Americans and the situation became critical until reinforcements arrived and the paratroopers were able to secure a position around the bridge. Three kilometres away, near a bridge over the River Merderet, there is still a remarkably well preserved roadside fox-hole that was used by the American General James Gavin. In Chef-du-Pont there are memorials to the 508th Parachute Regiment. On the war memorial in the cemetery near the church there is a plaque to honour Captain Rex Combs who commanded the men who gained control of the bridge over the River Merderet and on the road leading from the town a board commemorating Captain Roy Creek and the men of the 507th Parachute Infantry Regiment who also took part in capturing the bridge.

A flooded area around the River Merderet as it would have appeared in June 1944.

General Gavin's foxhole; (inset) General James Gavin.

Cherbourg

The assault on Cherbourg, a strategically important fortified port at the head of the Contentin Peninsula, began on 22 June 1944 and the city finally fell to American divisions commanded by General J. Lawton Collins on 30 June 1944. The German defenders, totalling 21,000 under Lieutenant General Karl-Wilhelm von Schlieben, had earlier rejected an offer to surrender and began to carry out demolitions that would delay the use of the port by the Allies. The eight day battle for Cherbourg left the city in a devastated condition so that the port's facilities could not be used until late July.

Cherbourg when it finally fell to the Americans in 1944.

The modern city of Cherbourg as it appears today.

After the battle, German prisoners being marched along the Avenue de Paris to captivity.

Today, the same place name remains on the wall.

An American soldier stands guard by the statue of Napoleon I still surrounded by German signposts.

Cherbourg's famous statue as it appears today.

German soldiers
resting close to
the city's Trinity
Church during
the occupation.

Colleville-Montgomery

Colleville-Montgomery Plage and Colleville-Montgomery were originally just plain Colleville but, after the war, they were renamed in honour of the commander-in-chief of the Allied land forces on D-Day, Field Marshall Bernard Montgomery, later Viscount Montgomery of Alamein.

On D-Day, the coastal resort of Colleville Plage was the centre of 'Queen Sector' of Sword Beach. After a heavy air and naval bombardment, the 3rd British Division came ashore led by the 1st South Lancashire and 2nd East Yorkshire Regiments. Behind the beaches there were two German strong points, 'Morris' and 'Hillman', and, although the Germans defending 'Morris' quickly surrendered, those at 'Hillman' offered strong resistance. This led to some delay until the arrival of the 1st Suffolk Regiment when, supported by the tanks of the Royal Hussars and Staffordshire Yeomanry, they pressed forward and succeeded in storming the German positions.

The remains of the two German strong points can be reached by following a road now called Rue du Suffolk Regiment. Along the landing beaches are memorials dedicated to '*des premiers Allies tombes le 6 juin 1944*' and to Field Marshal Montgomery and Commandant Philippe Kieffer, commander of the French Commandos.

British soldiers enter Colleville-Montgomery.

The German strong points at Colleville-Montgomery as they appear today.

A L'AUBE DU 6 JUIN 1944
SUR CETTE PLAGE
DEBARQUENT LES
FUSILIERS MARINS FRANÇAIS
DU COMMANDANT
PHILIPPE KIEFFER
COMMANDO
BRITANNIQUE N° 4

A memorial that recalls the contribution of Commandant Kieffer and the French Commandos.

The statue of Field Marshall Montgomery.

An impressive memorial that recalls the landings on Sword Beach.

In 2008, veterans returned to pay their respects to their fallen comrades.

Courseulles-sur-Mer

Courselles-sur-Mer, a fishing port famous for its oyster beds, lies at the mouth of the River Seulles and midway between Arromanches-les-Bains and Ouistreham. On D-Day, the town lay in the centre of Juno Beach and was the landing area allocated to the 3rd Canadian Infantry Division under Major-General Rodney Keller.

They were led ashore by the Royal Regina Rifles and the 1st Canadian Scottish Regiment. Unfortunately, most of the amphibious tanks of the First Hussars that were launched 4 kilometres out to sea sank but those that reached the shore immediately opened fire on the German positions. Elsewhere, the prevailing tides and offshore rocks made landing difficult and, since the town was well fortified, once ashore the Canadian infantry became involved in fierce street fighting before the town was finally liberated late in the afternoon. By the evening of 6 June, 21,000 men and 3,200 vehicles had been successfully landed on Juno Beach. On entering the town and on the west bank of the River Seulles is a large Cross of Lorraine that celebrates the return of General de Gaulle to France in June 1944. On the seafront on the east bank of the river there is a Sherman tank named 'Bold' which originally belonged to the Canadian Armoured Regiment (First Hussars). This was recovered 4 kilometres out to sea and, once restored, became a memorial dedicated to the men of the regiment that lost their lives on D-Day. Nearby, another memorial marks the place where General de Gaulle landed on 14 June on his way to Bayeux. On the sides of the steps leading to the beach there are memorials to Regina Rifle Regiment and the 1st Canadian Scottish Regiment. To the east of the town is a large dagger-shaped memorial to the Royal Winnipeg Rifles, nicknamed the 'Little Black Devils'. It was erected in June 1964 to mark the twentieth anniversary of D-Day.

The impressive Juno Beach Centre, a museum and cultural centre, which was opened in June 2003.

Courselles-sur-Mer today.

Creully

Fourteen kilometres to the east of Bayeux lies the town of Creully. On D-Day, the 4th/7th Royal Dragoon Guards, who had earlier landed on Gold Beach, met no resistance and occupied the town without opposition. The town, which overlooks the River Seulles, was later to become famous when General Montgomery established his Tactical Headquarters in a caravan parked in the grounds of the impressive Château Creullet. The same location was also used by correspondents of the BBC and other nations to broadcast news of events in Normandy. Later, Montgomery was to entertain Winston Churchill, the South African general, Jan Smuts, and, later, King George VI, General de Gaulle and General Eisenhower in the grand salon of the castle.

On the outskirts of the town is a memorial to the 4th/7th Royal Dragoon Guards and outside the town's church is a statue dedicated to the memory of the citizens of Creully who lost their lives in the First and Second World Wars. Situated in the town's square is the town hall that houses a commemorative plaque to Royal Engineers that reads: 'During the critical days of June and July 1944, the world listened to news of the Battle of Normandy broadcast by radio correspondents of many nations from the BBC studio in the tower of this castle.'

Approaching Creully with the château in the background.

The Château Creullet.

A memorial to the citizens of Creully who lost their lives during the First and Second World Wars.

General Montgomery with visitors to his Tactical Headquarters in the grounds of the château.

The centre of the town of Creully today.

Crisbecq

The only heavy battery on the eastern coast of the Contentin Peninsula was at Crisbecq. Located 2½ kilometres from the shore on the crest of a hill overlooking Utah Beach, its guns covered the coastline between St Vaast-la-Hougue to Grandcamp-Maisy. Originally built by the slave labourers employed by the Todt organisation, in June 1944 it had not been fully completed, but with three long range guns in concrete positions, numerous bunkers and a garrison of 400 men, it was still the important keystone of this stretch of the Atlantic Wall. Early in April 1944, the Allies bombed the battery and the day before D-Day nearly 600 tons of bombs were dropped on the site. Unrecognisable but with its guns still intact, it managed to sink an American destroyer and hold out for several days. In the end, it was necessary for the 4th Infantry Division to engage in hand-to-hand fighting and the Crisbecq battery was finally captured on the morning of 12 June. For a while, the fierce German resistance, led by Oberleutnant Walter Omhsen, had succeeded in holding up the American advance inland. Although dynamited by American engineers after its capture, today much of the battery remains intact. From the top it is possible to have a panoramic view of the coastline towards Utah Beach.

One of the guns of the Crisbecq battery after it had finally fallen to the Americans.

A gun emplacement of the Crisbecq as it appears today.

Douvres La Délivrande

On D-Day, Douvres La Délivrande, midway between Juno and Sword Beaches, was particularly important since it was the site of a Wasserman, a long range German radar device. The first attempts of the 51st Highland Division to take the installation met with fierce resistance and failed. Other attempts were also unsuccessful and it was not until 17 June that men of the 41st Royal Marine Commando, aided by the Churchill tanks of the 22nd Dragoons, managed to overcome German resistance and the eleven day struggle came to an end. Today, on the outskirts of the town, it is still possible to see parts of the former bunker system.

Off the road leading to Caen, in a picturesque wooded area, is the La Délivrande War Cemetery. It contains 1,123 graves of which 927 are British, 180 German and 11 Canadian. Most of the graves are of men who lost their lives in the various battles fought between the coast and Caen. The graves include those of six lieutenant generals, the Reverend Cameron Carnegie, a twenty-seven-year-old Army chaplain from Edinburgh who was attached to the Royal Army Service Corps and died as the result of an accident and Major David de Symons Barrow of the Queen's Royal Regiment who was the son of General Sir George de Symons Barrow. Sixty-three of the burials are of unidentified servicemen.

The remains of the German radar station.

What remains of the radar station and German bunkers today.

The British war cemetery at Douvres La Délivrande.

In the churchyard of the town's Notre-Dame de la Délivrande is the grave of Sergeant Denholm Jackson, a New Zealander who served with the Royal New Zealand Air Force and lost his life in April 1943.

Escoville

Escoville lies on the east bank of the River Orne and to the south of the villages of Hérouvillette and Le Mesnil. On D-Day, the whole area along the east bank of the River Orne was the scene of bitter fighting involving the 3rd and 5th Parachute Brigades whilst the 8th Parachute Battalion had landed to the south of Escoville with the aim of destroying the bridges over the River Dives at Bures and Troarn. Although Escoville was liberated on 7 June, a fierce counter-attack by the 21st Panzer Division forced the British forces to withdraw and the town was not finally taken until 18 July at the start of Operation *Goodwood*.

In front of the L'Eglise Saint Laurent, there is a memorial to 'Our British liberators' and, just outside the village, a monument dedicated to the 8th Parachute Battalion inscribed: 'In memory of all ranks of the Battalion who fought and died for freedom.' In the communal churchyard beside the church there is the solitary grave of twenty-two-year-old Private William Wilkins from Kingswood, Gloucestershire, who lost his life on 7 June. Close to the village, Colonel Henry Sweeney (nicknamed Tod Sweeney) saved the life of a wounded corporal and was subsequently awarded a Military Cross for his bravery.

Fontenay-Le-Pesnel

Lying some 16 kilometres to the west of Caen, during late June and July 1944 the area around Fonteney-Le-Pesnel witnessed very heavy fighting. Here, on 25 June, 49th Infantry Division faced a German front line held by an infantry battalion of the Panzer-Lehr Division. Although the German positions were overcome, men of the Hitlerjugend Division counter-attacked and reclaimed the position. However, the following day British infantry drove the Germans back and finally occupied Fontenay-Le-Pesnel.

A kilometre to the south-east of the village lies Fontenay-le-Pesnel War Cemetery. It contains the graves of 519 men – 546 British, 4 Canadian and 59 German. The British dead include members of the Royal Warwickshire, the Durham Light Infantry, the East Lancashire and the South Staffordshire regiments. At the entrance to the cemetery is an impressive memorial dedicated to the 49th (West Riding) Division. The grave of twenty-two-year-old Private Frank Kelly who came from Plymouth and was serving in the Royal Warwicks carries an epitaph requested by his parents – 'Beneath foreign soil our darling son is laid but in our hearts his memory is forever engraved'.

Men of the 7th Reconnaissance Regiment, 17th Duke of York's Royal Canadian Hussars amidst the ruins of Escoville.

A captured German tank in good condition captured at Fonteney-Le-Pesnel.

The Fonteney-Le-Pesnel War Cemetery.

The memorial to the 49th (West Riding) Division at the entrance to the cemetery.

Grandcamp-Maisy and Pointe Du Hoc

On the Normandy coast between Vierville-sur-Mer and Isigny-sur-Mer, Grandcamp-Maisy is situated to the west of the American landings on Omaha Beach and close the Pointe du Hoc. After landing on Omaha Beach and storming the headland, the Pointe du Hoc, the Americans bypassed Grandcamp-Maisy, and overcame stiff opposition offered by the German 352nd Infantry Division to reach Isigny-sur-Mer.

Near the entrance to Grandcamp-Maisy, amongst the ruins of a church destroyed during the fighting, is a communal cemetery that contains the grave of Flying Officer Nicholas Peel. The son of a Wiltshire clergyman, the Spitfire pilot was shot down in November 1941. Close by is the grave of the highly decorated leader of the French Commandos, Philippe Kieffer. Shortly before his father entered Paris with the Free French Forces, his son, Claude, was killed fighting for the *Maquis*, the French Resistance. Amongst many memorials in the town is a *Musee des Rangers*, a memorial to Guyenne and Tunisie Squadrons of the French Air Force and an impressive statue of peace.

Philippe Kieffer. Born in Haiti in 1899, he first worked in a bank in New York but in 1929, Kieffer enlisted in the French Navy. A year later, after the surrender of France, he crossed to Britain, joined the Free French and in 1941 formed the French Marine Commandos. In June 1944, his men landed on Sword Beach and fought alongside the British units. Kieffer was twice wounded but was soon able to rejoin his unit and was the first member of the Free French forces to enter Paris. During his military career he was awarded the French *Croix de Guerre* and the British Military Cross.

The grave of Philippe Kieffer in Grandcamp-Maisy.

A memorial to the squadrons of the French Air Forces that served with RAF Bomber Command.

The Statue of Peace.

The Pointe du Hoc is a forbidding spur of land that the Germans considered unassailable. To the west of the US landing beaches at Omaha, before the war it was a popular beauty spot that had commanding views both east and west along the coast and, because of this, the Germans converted it into a strong point. On D-Day, the German positions were heavily bombarded by US and British battleships before the headland was stormed by three companies of specially trained men that were part of Lieutenant Colonel James Rudder's 2nd Ranger Battalion. Using climbing equipment and displaying outstanding courage whilst under heavy German fire, they climbed the cliffs only to find the gun emplacements empty. The next day, the Rangers discovered the guns some distance inland beyond the coast road and destroyed them. In all, the Rangers suffered 135 casualties, over half their total.

Today, the 12 hectares of coastal land is preserved and, amongst the craters, there remains evidence of the shattered bunkers. There are numerous memorials and plaques in the memory of the 2nd Rangers Battalion and in June 1979, the area passed into the care of the American Battle Monuments Commission.

US soldiers of the 2nd Ranger Battalion begin to scale the Point du Hoc.

The Point du Hoc today.

Graye-sur-Mer

On D-Day, Graye-sur-Mer was on the edge of Mike Sector of Juno Beach and like most of the Normandy coastline, the Germans saw to it that it was protected by barbed wire, mines and concrete pillboxes. At 7.45 a.m. on the morning of 6 June, 7th Canadian Brigade which included the Royal Winnipeg Rifles known as the 'Little Black Devils' and the 6th Armoured Regiment came ashore accompanied by the 26th Assault Squadron of the Royal Engineers. The immediate problem they faced was that the exit from the beach was blocked by an anti-tank ditch and a flooded culvert connected to the River Seulles. To remedy this, a Churchill AVRE tank went forward to fill the anti-tank ditch with 2 tons of logs. Unfortunately, a second tank slowly slid under the water where it remained with additional rubble until it was all concreted over. After murderous hand-to-hand fighting, the arrival of the tanks of the 1st Hussars Regiment won the day and Graye-sur-Mer was liberated.

Today, there is a *Comité du Débarquement* memorial on the dunes at Graye-sur-Mer and near it the Churchill tank fell into the culvert all those years ago. Recovered in 1976, after renovation it became a memorial to George Dunn, the tank's original driver.

Elsewhere, the coast contains the remains of numerous German bunkers as well as memorials to the Royal Winnipeg Rifles and the Inns of Court Regiment.

Bedecked with poppies, the 'One Charlie' Churchill tank that on D-Day was left stranded on the beach.

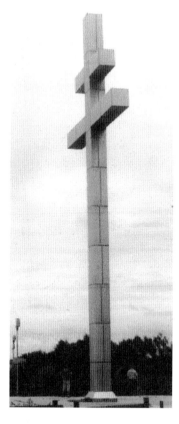

The Croix de Lorraine.

A monument dedicated to the Inns of Court Armoured Regiment.

The *Comité du Débarquement* memorial.

The quiet seaside resort that is Graye-sur-Mer today.

Hermanville-sur-Mer

On 6 June, Hermanville-sur-Mer lay just behind Sword beach and was liberated by units of the British 3rd Army under General Tom Rennie as they advanced inland from the coast. At 9 a.m., men from the 1st South Lancashire Regiment and 2nd King's Own Shropshire Light Infantry entered the village to be greeted by cheering local civilians and the encouraging sight of groups of German prisoners-of-war being escorted in the opposite direction.

Along the seafront of Hermanville-sur-Mer there are numerous plaques and memorials. These are dedicated to the 23rd Destroyer Flotilla, the Royal Artillary, the 3rd Infantry Division, the South Lancashire Regiment and the Royal Coomandos.

To the north of the village lies Hermanville War Cemetery that contains the graves of 1,005 Allied soldiers of which all but nineteen are British. These include Lt-Col. David Board, Lt-Col. Richard Buberry and two Army chaplains – Peter Firth from Scorton in Lancashire and Henry Wagg from Lancing in Sussex. Also buried in the cemetery is Private Kenneth Graham.

Private Kenneth Graham's real name was Kurt Wilhelm Gumpertz, and was from a German Jewish family that came to Britain as refugees from Hitler's Nazi regime. At the start of the war, men from Germany, Austria, Poland and Czechoslovakia and other Eastern European countries under German occupation volunteered to join the British Army. As it was known that they could only expect the harshest treatment if they were taken prisoner, they were provided with false names, identity disks and papers. Kurt Grumpertz first served in the Hampshire Regiment but later transferred to No. 3 (X) Group of No. 10 (Inter-Allied) Commando, a unit consisted of men from various European backgrounds under the command of Captain Brian Hylton-Jones. They fought bravely and the X Troop lost twenty-one men killed and twenty-two wounded to become amongst the highest casualty rates in the British Army. Kurt Gumpertz lost his life on 12 June 1944.

Hill 112 – 'Cornwall Hill'

Close to Caen and in a commanding position, Hill 112 was the scene of some of the most ferocious fighting of the whole of the Normandy campaign. The Germans appreciated the position that gave every advantage to the defenders when they claimed that 'he who controls Hill 112 controls Normandy'. In the monumental struggle, time and time again ground was taken by one side and then recaptured by the other. During two days of fighting between 10 and 11 July, the 43rd (Wessex) Division under Major-General Hubert Essame included men from the Dorset and Hampshire regiments as well as the Duke of Cornwall's Light Infantry. On the Hill, they faced the battle hardened men of the 9th and 10th SS Panzers and some of the best German infantry units fighting in Normandy. During this period the British suffered two thousand casualties and the Hill became the site of shell craters, corpses, wrecked vehicles and the blazing remains of tanks. Hill 112 was not finally taken until 3 August and was to contribute much to the final Allied victory in Normandy. During the struggle for Hill

Major-General T. G. Rennie. Born in 1900 in Foochow in China and the son of a doctor, Tom Rennie was educated at Loretto School and, after leaving Sandhurst Royal Military Academy, was commissioned in the Black Watch. In 1940, he was taken prisoner by the Germans in France but managed to escape and make his way home. Two years later, at El Alamein, he was awarded the DSO. After commanding the British 3rd Army on D-Day, he was involved in the British advance across France and Belgium and was eventually killed in action in 1945 whilst crossing the River Rhine.

British troops passing through Hermanville-sur-Mer on D-Day.

Memorials and plaques along the seafront at Hermanville-sur-Mer.

The Hermanville-sur-Mer War Cemetery.

112, the 5th Battalion of the Duke of Cornwall's Light Infantry suffered 320 casualties with only one man taken prisoner. After the battle, ninety-three of them men from the battalion that had lost their lives were buried on the Hill so that, not surprisingly, the Hill came to be known as 'Cornwall Hill'.

Some of the verses of a poem written by one of the survivors who returned to the scene of the battle, Cyril Onions, sums up the feelings of those involved:

A memorial to men of the 5th Battalion of the Duke of Cornwall's Light Infantry.

Hill 112 in its true rural setting as it appears today.

Hill 112 had always been a field of corn,
A place where young men had fought and died;
Young men who had children, yet unborn,
Gallant men, who's enemy lay side by side.

I had seen these men, in booted feet,
Marching so proudly, in British lane
Now they lay in graves so neat,
With loved ones standing in silent pain.

Today, Hill 112 still dominates the area but it has returned to its former rural setting with several monuments that recall the events of July 1944. By the roadside there is a monument dedicated to the men of the 43rd Wessex Division whilst the road that leads to the top of the hill and is close to the wood where so many died later became known as the 'Crown of thorns'. It is a place that has atmosphere and where visitors can still find rusting bullets and shrapnel in the fields.

Hottot-les-Bagues

Hottot-les-Bagues lies to the south-east of Bayeux and was in an area where the Hampshire Regiment faced the Panzer Lehr Division, reckoned to be amongst the best in the German Army. On 14 July, the town was finally liberated by the British 50th Infantry Division.

Close by is the Hottot-les-Bagues War Cemetery that contains 1,137 graves of which 965 are British and Commonwealth and 132 German. Those buried in the cemetery were mainly brought from the surrounding district at a time when the Allied forces were beginning an encircling movement towards Caen. Those in the cemetery include a large number of men of the Royal Tank Corps, the Duke of Wellington (West Riding) Regiment and the Scots Guards. The cemetery includes the graves of a number of eighteen-year-old British soldiers including Privates Stanley Franklin and Lionel Evans of the Somerset Light Infantry, Harold Stannard of the Green Howards, Ronald Pilkington of the Durham Light Infantry and Kenneth Greenwood of the Duke of Wellington (West Riding) Regiment. Amongst senior officers buried in the cemetery are Brigadier John Mackintosh-Walker and Brigadier James Hargest. Both had previously been awarded the DSO and MC and whilst Mackintosh commanded the 227th (Highland) Brigade and was killed in action on 17 July, Hargest, a New Zealander, who was also a veteran of the First World War, served in the New Zealand Infantry.

Above and below: The entrance to the Hottot-les-Bagues War Cemetery.

Isigny-sur-Mer

Isigny-sur-Mer lies at the southern end of the Contentin Peninsula close to the border between Maches and Calvados. Before the war the town was famous for its dairy produce. It was intended that the US 29th Infantry Division commanded by Brigadier-General Norman Cota would liberate the town on D-Day but because of the hold up on Omaha Beach, this was not possible. On the night of 8/9 June, Isigny-sur-Mer was subjected to a US naval bombardment that destroyed most of the buildings in the town. This was to prove unnecessary since the following day American troops faced no resistance when they entered the town.

On 14 June, General de Gaulle arrived and addressed the French people recently freed from German occupation. A *Comité du Débarquement* monument now marks the place where he spoke.

American vehicles in the devastated town.

La Cambe and Orglandes – German War Cemeteries

In Normandy there are eighteen Second World War cemeteries supervised by the Commonwealth War Graves Commission. In addition there are six German war cemeteries containing 77,960 graves. These are at Champigny St Andre, Mariguy, Mont de Huisnes, St Desir Le Lisieux, La Cambe and Orglandes. There are also 2,300 German war graves to be found in British war cemeteries. During the war, local French people that came across dead German soldiers tended to bury them in fields and there are probably many that have yet to be discovered.

La Cambe lies close to Bayeux and contains 21,222 German war graves of which 207 are of unknown identity. The site was originally an American war cemetery but, in 1961, the bodies of the US soldiers were either sent home or transferred to the cemetery overlooking Omaha Beach at Colleville-sur-Mer. It was then taken over by the *Volksbund Deutsche Kriegsgraberfursorge*, the German War Graves Commission, and its cemetery. Since that time, the bodies of an additional 700 Germans have been found in former Normandy battlefields and added to those already interred there. The majority of the Germans buried at La Cambe lost their lives during June, July and August 1944 and their ages range from 16 to 72. One of those buried there is the tank battle ace, Michael Wittmann, whose body was not discovered until 1983.

La Cambe German War Cemetery.

The entrance to Orglandes German War Cemetery.

Michael Wittmann, the son of a farmer, was born in 1914 in the village of Vogelthal in Bavaria. He joined the German Army in 1934 and his first experience of action came five years later when the Germans invaded Poland. As his reputation grew as a tank commander, during the campaign against Russia on the Eastern Front he was commissioned and held the rank of SS-*Unterstürmfuhrer* and in 1943, after the Battle of Kursk, Wittmann was awarded the Iron Cross. By D-Day, he held the rank of SS-*Oberstürmfuhrer* and was placed in command of a company of the 1st SS Panzer Corps where he again did well as his Tiger tanks battled against the US Shermans. On 8 August 1944, he was killed close to the town of Saint-Aignan-de-Cramesnil. Afterwards there was much speculation regarding the responsibility for his death with men of the 1st Northamptonshire Yeomanry, the 4th Canadian Armoured Division, the 144 Regiment Royal Armoured Corps and the RAF Second Tactical Air Force all making claims. All the claims have been discredited and so the mystery remains.

Even today, the bodies of war casualties are still being found though formal burial ceremonies now seldom occur. La Cambe war cemetery is dominated by a cenotaph-like grass mound surmounted by a large stone cross with two engraved figures at its side. The two figures represent grieving parents and beneath the grass mound lie the bodies of 296 largely unknown German casualties.

Michael Wittmann.

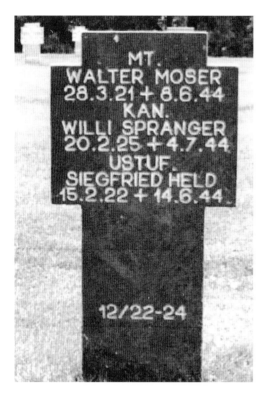

Typical graves found in German war cemeteries.

Unlike British war cemetery headstones of upright white stone, most German headstones are grey and placed flat on the ground but there are also some that are upright. Each is engraved with the names of three or four German soldiers buried beneath.

Orglandes War Cemetery lies close to a village of the same name to the west of Bayeux. Situated in an attractive rural setting, it contains the graves of 10,152 German soldiers.

Langrune-sur-Mer

Situated at the point where Juno and Sword Beaches join, on D-Day no landing was planned at Langrune-sur-Mer since it was intended that the 48th Royal Marine Commando advancing from the west would link up with 41st Royal Commando advancing from Lion-sur-Mer to the east. Unfortunately, strong German resistance prevented this from happening since the gap between the two bridgeheads developed into a weakness that the German 21st Panzer Division hoped to exploit.

However, after a naval bombardment, British Commandos advancing from St Aubin liberated the town on 7 June.

British landing
craft approaching
Langrune-sur-Mer
on 7 June.

The impressive thirteenth-century church close to the centre of Langrune-sur-Mer.

Lion-sur-Mer

At 8.45 a.m. on D-Day, the 41st Royal Marine Commando was first ashore at Lion-sur-Mer followed by men of the 1st Battalion of the South Lancashire Regiment. They were fiercely resisted by the German 736 Infantry Regiment and the British suffered heavy casualties. Since it was in an area where Juno and Sword Beaches met, the Germans thought that this might be a weakness which they could exploit. In spite of being subject to heavy air and naval bombardment, the Germans held on stubbornly but were forced to surrender the town the following day.

Just off the front there are two squares. One, the *Place du 18 Juin 1940*, recalls General de Gaulle's call to the French people from London on that day; the other, the *Place du 41 Royal Marine*, commemorates the landing of the British commandos on D-Day. Close to the beach there is a memorial on a plaque supported by two pillars dedicated to *aux soldiers allies et aux civiles tombes pour notre liberte*.

The memorial to the soldiers and civilians who gave their lives for freedom.

British troops coming ashore at Lion-sur-Mer on D-Day.

The liberation of the town the following day.

Longues-sur-Mer

To the west of Arromanches-les-Bains and just beyond Manvieux lies the village of Longues-sur-Mer. In 1943, close to the village the Germans began to construct a naval battery consisting of four guns, anti-aircraft guns, searchlights and machine-gun emplacements that would present a threat to an approaching invasion fleet. The Longue battery was to become an important part of the German Atlantic Wall. The battery was finally completed during April 1944. At first it was manned by the German navy but was later transferred to the German Army. On the morning of D-Day, the battery was bombarded by the British battleships HMS *Ajax* and HMS *Argonaut* and put out of action. Later in the day, it resumed firing until it was silenced by the French cruiser *George Leygues* and the US battleship, *Arkansas*. By the evening three of the battery's four guns had been disabled but the fourth continued to operate until 7 p.m. The next day, the battery surrendered to British troops advancing from Arromanches.

Luc-sur-Mer

Long before D-Day, Luc-sur-Mer had been the target of a British commando raid. On the night of 27 September 1941, the 5th Troop of No. 1 Commando carried out a raid on the town. Several commandos were injured and two died on the beach and these were buried with full military honours by the Germans.

One of the shattered German guns at Longues-sur-Mer.

The graves of the men who died during the commando raid in September 1941. They include Elwyn Edwards, formerly of the Royal Welch Fusiliers, and Cyril Evans, formerly of the South Wales Borderers. The third grave is that of Squadron Leader James Hill whose Wellington bomber was shot down on 18 September 1940.

Men of 46 Royal Marine Commando enter Luc-sur-Mer on 7 June 1944.

A memorial on the seafront at Luc-sur-Mer that commemorates both the Commando action of September 1941 and the liberation of the town on 7 June 1944.

There was no landing on the beach of the Luc-sur-Mer on D-Day, but the following morning the town was liberated by 46 Royal Marine Commando who faced little opposition.

Merville-Franceville

High above the coast, overlooking the estuary of the River Orne and close to the village of Merville, the Germans had built an impressive gun battery that could, on D-Day, be ranged on Sword Beach. The Merville battery consisted of four bomb-proof vaulted concrete casemates and bunkers to accommodate men and store ammunition. Visited by Field Marshal Rommel in May 1944, it was clearly in the interests of the British invasion forces that the battery be eliminated. Aware that it would be strongly defended, the unit assigned to remove the threat was the 9th (Eastern and Home Counties) Parachute Battalion part of the 3rd Parachute Brigade commanded by Lieutenant Colonel Terence Otway and the 591st Parachute Squadron, Royal Engineers. The episode began with a series of disasters. Soon after midnight on D-Day, an RAF Lancaster bomber mistook the nearby village of Gonneville for the battery and completely destroyed the homes of the local community. Soon afterwards the British paratroopers were dropped some distance from their intended landing area and this led to confusion. Then, when the troop bearing gliders arrived, their tow-ropes

Field Marshal Erwin Rommel visiting the Merville Battery on 6 May 1944.

broke and they disappeared into the waters of the English Channel. By 2.30 a.m., only 150 men had reached their pre-arranged assembly point. When the main force finally arrived at 4.30 a.m., they too landed some distance away and had to make their way to the agreed assembly point. Once the assault on the German positions began there was hand-to-hand fighting between the paratroopers and German gunners with the British suffering heavy casualties. The German battery commander was twenty-four-year-old Oberleutnant Raimund Steiner. An Austrian by birth, his family were known to be anti-Nazi and his father was destined to die in a concentration camp. On the morning of 6 June the position was still uncertain and the paratroopers again attacked the battery, this time with the assistance of the RAF and the guns of the Royal Navy the German positions were finally overrun and afterwards it was discovered that the guns only had a range of four miles and it would have been impossible for them to be used against those landing at Sword Beach.

After the battery had been captured, the British withdrew and this allowed the Germans to re-occupy the position. On 7 June, commandos again assaulted the German positions but were forced to withdraw. The British never succeeded in completely destroying the battery and it remained under German control until 17 August. During the operation, the British suffered some 600 casualties and the Germans only 130, understandably today there is some disagreement between military historians as to the success of the raid!

Today, all four gun positions remain in reasonably good condition and one has been carefully restored and is now a museum. In nearby Merville churchyard there are the graves of six British airmen whose Lancaster bomber was shot down on 18 April 1943. They are buried in one plot but unfortunately, since only one member of the crew was identified and another was missing, it was been impossible to list all their names on the headstone.

A gun emplacement of the Merville Battery as it appears today.

Above and below: The rival commanders
– Lt-Col. Otway and Lt Steiner.

A memorial to Lt-Col. Otway at the site of the battery.

A ceremony held in 2009 to commemorate the 65th anniversary of the struggle for the Merville Battery.

Montebourg

During the American advance along the Contentin Peninsula after their landing on Utah Beach, one of the obstacles to reaching Cherbourg was the heavily defended town of Montebourg. There the American 4th Division and 82nd Airborne Division under General Raymond Barton faced General Karl-Wilhel von Schlieben's 243rd Division that was determined to hold the town of Montebourg and so prevent the Allies from reaching and using the port of Cherbourg. The battle raged for several days, during which time the town was reduced to rubble. When the town was finally liberated on 20 June American forces entered the town to discover that Von Schlieben had withdrawn his forces in order to help with the defence of Cherbourg.

Even though some 90 per cent of the buildings of the town were destroyed, the scars of war have long disappeared and a splendid new town has risen from the ashes of the old. Today, there is plaque in the remains of the old sixteenth-century castle dedicated to the men of the 4th American Infantry Division who lost their lives in the battle to liberate Montebourg.

General Raymond Barton.

The ruins of Montebourg after the battle for the town.

The Church of St Jacques situated close to the centre of the town.

Pegasus Bridge

At a few minutes past midnight on 6 June 1944, men of the 2nd (Airborne) Battalion of the Oxfordshire and Buckinghamshire Light Infantry that was part of the 6th Airborne Division under Major John Howard landed near the two bridges over the Caen Canal and River Orne in six Horsa gliders. They were the first Allied troops to set foot on French soil on D-Day. The glider carrying Major Howard landed only 60 metres from the bridge, the second a short distance behind and the third between them. Known as Operation *Deadstick*, their task was to seize the two bridges and hold them until assistance arrived. Both bridges were captured within minutes of landing but the German garrison, under Major Hans Schmidt, soon began to fight back. Lieutenant Den Brotheridge led the first charge to capture the bridge across the canal but was wounded and died shortly afterwards. It is claimed that he was the first Allied casualty on D-Day but this is sometimes disputed.

On the morning of D-Day, Lord Lovat's 1st Special Service Brigade had landed at Ouistreham and, after liberating the town, advanced inland to join up with 6th British Airborne Division. The capture of the bridges was essential and, when the commandos arrived, fighting was still going on. Even so, Lovat and his men followed Piper Bill

Commandos crossing the bridge later in the day.

The Horsa gliders at Pegasus Bridge.

Some of the heroes of Pegasus Bridge (left to right): Major John Howard, Lord Lovat and Piper Bill Millin, with Lt Den Brotheridge (lower left).

The Gondree café today.

Pegasus, the winged horse of Greek mythology.

Pegasus as the emblem of the Airborne Forces.

Pegasus Bridge and the Gondree café as they appear today.

Millin playing 'Highland Laddie' and 'The Road to the Isles' and went forward across the bridge. After the bridges had been taken, they helped to reinforce the defensive positions and fought off ferocious German counter-attacks. Earlier that morning, Georges Gondree and his wife, Therese, the proprietors of a café close to the canal bridge, had emerged from their cellar to produce bottles of champagne for the troops and allow their home to become a medical aid post.

The bridge over the canal came to be known as Pegasus Bridge and was named after the famous winged horse of Greek mythology that had become the emblem of the Airborne Forces. Today the area is a major tourist attraction and it is still possible to enjoy refreshments at the Gondree Café. There are many plaques and monuments that recall the events of 6 June 1944 as well as a splendid new museum.

Tourists visit the memorials that mark the place where the gliders landed on 6 June 1944.

The museum and memorial at Pegasus Bridge.

Port-en-Bessin

A fishing port to the west of Arromanches and situated on the western limit of Gold Beach, on D-Day, Port-en-Besin did not lie in any designated landing area and it was not until 7 June that 47 Royal Marine Commando moved to liberate the town. The previous day they had experienced a difficult time when they landed at Le Hamel but, on that day as they faced the crack German 352nd Infantry Division, their efforts were backed by a naval bombardment and strikes from rocket-firing RAF Typhoons. After taking two German strong points, the Commandos faced determined German counter-attacks and house-to-house fighting continued into the evening. On the morning of 8 June the Germans finally surrendered.

Soon afterwards, they linked up with the US 1st Infantry Division advancing from Omaha Beach. Afterwards Port-en-Bessin became an important PLUTO (Pipe Line Under The Ocean) port and large oil storage facilities were built on the outskirts of the town.

At the exit to the town, the Underwater Wrecks Museum that contains the remains of many tanks and vehicles found under the water and close to the D-Day beaches.

British troops advance on Port-en-Bessin.

Port-en-Bessin today.

Ranville

Ranville lied to the south-east of Pegasus Bridge and was the main dropping area of the 6th Airborne Division on D-Day. The division consisted of the 3rd and 5th Parachute Brigades and the glider borne troops of the 6th Air Landing Brigade. Whilst the men of the 3rd Parachute Brigade were attacking the Merville battery (see pages XX), the 5th Brigade was preparing the area around Ranville for the arrival of a large force of gliders. Their first task was to clear away 'Rommel's asparagus' – a large number of spaced poles intended to hinder airborne landings – and then act as 'Pathfinders' by marking the proposed landing area with flares. Under the command of Major-General Richard Gale, the first Allied general to set foot on liberated French soil, the vast armada of Horsa gliders began to land at 3.30 a.m. They brought with them anti-tank guns and jeeps. Of interest, the major-general's glider was piloted by S. C. 'Billy' Griffith, a Sussex and England wicket-keeper. By morning, the area was a mass of men milling around whole and broken gliders.

Today, the grass square close to the town's church is called *Place General Sir Richard Gale* and, in the town, on a wall in the *Place du 6 Juin 1944* is a plaque that commemorates that fact that Ranville was the first French town to be liberated on 6 June by the 13th (Lancashire) Battalion of the Parachute Regiment. The church contains a stained glass window dedicated to the 6th Airborne Division.

Ranville War Cemetery lies close to the centre of the town and contains the graves of 2,562 men – 2,151 British, 322 German and 76 Canadian – who mostly died during 6–7 June 1944. Amongst the many interesting burials are those of the Canadian brothers, Lieutenants Maurice and Philippe Rousseau, a sixteen-year-old Portsmouth boy, Private Robert Johns, who served in the Parachute Regiment, Private Emile Corteil, who is buried with his paratroop dog, 'Glen' and Kurt Meyer, a German Jew who served under the assumed name Peter Moody in No. 10 Inter-Allied Commando. Close to the wall in the in the neighbouring churchyard lies Lieutenant Den Brotheridge.

Congestion and accidents as Horsa gliders land near Ranville.

Ranville War Cemetery.

The crowded churchyard at Ranville.

Private Emile Corteil and his dog, 'Glen'.

The grave of sixteen-year-old Private Robert Johns.

Ryes

Five kilometres in land from Arromanches, the village of Ryes was liberated by the 1st Battalion of the Dorset Regiment on the afternoon of D-Day. Some 2 kilometres from Ryes and close to Bazenville is the Ryes War Cemetery which contains the graves of 979 servicemen who lost their lives on D-Day or soon afterwards.

Of these 630 are British, 326 German, 21 Canadian, and an Australian and a Pole. These include the graves of thirteen merchant seamen of the SS *Empire Rosebery* that struck a mine off Arromanches on 24 August 1944 and sank. There are also members of the crew of HMS *Glen Avon*, a minesweeper that had in 1940 rescued hundreds of British soldiers from the beaches of Dunkirk but, on 2 September 1944, sank during a gale off Arromanches.

Ryes War Cemetery.

St Aubin-sur-Mer

St Aubin-sur-Mer lies on the Normandy coast between Courseulles-sur-Mer and Langrune-sur-Mer. Situated on the edge of Juno Beach, on D-Day the town's seafront was strongly defended by the Germans but, after a naval bombardment, at 7.30 a.m. the 48 Royal Marine Commando made their way ashore. With the aid of the amphibious tanks of North Shore Regiment of Canada, after three hours of fighting, the town was liberated.

Today, there remains an intact German bunker on the seafront still displaying its 50-mm gun. There are also monuments dedicated to the 48 Royal Marine Commandos and the Canadian North Shore Regiment. Some distance away close to the offices of the *Syndicat d'Initiative* (information bureau) is another memorial that records that 'on these beaches at H Hour 6th June 1944 landed the amphibious tanks of the 10th Canadian Armoured Regiment (Fort Garry Horse)'.

A nearby plaque also recalls that on 4 August 1940, Maurice Duclos, a French secret agent code-named 'Saint Jacques', landed and made his way inland to help organise and fight with the resistance. He did this on several occasions and was awarded the Legion d'Honneur, La Croix de Guerre and from the British, an OBE and Military Cross. After the war, he lived in Argentina until his death in 1981.

An indication of the damage that occurred when the Allies landed at St Aubin-sur-Mer.

The German bunker that fired on Allied troops as they landed on the beach.

SUR CETTE PLAGE DE
SAINT-AUBIN AL'AUBE
DU 6 JUIN 1944 A 7.30
FUT ETABLIE UNE TÊTE
DE PONT PAR LE REGIMENT
D'INFANTERIE CANADIENNE
DES "NORTH SHORE",
OUVRANT LA VOIE AU
48 ème COMMANDO
DES "ROYAL MARINES"

Memorials on the seafront to 48 Royal Marine Commandos, Canadian North Shore Regiment and Maurice Duclos.

St Laurent-sur-Mer and the American Military Cemetery and Memorial

St Laurent-sur-Mer, a town that stretches up a hill, lies immediately behind Omaha Beach. The town contains a memorial to the United States 8th Engineer Special Brigade and, in front of an old German bunker, memorials to the US Second Infantry Division and Provisional Engineer Special Brigade Group. It is also close to the American Military Cemetery.

The American Military Cemetery and Memorial overlook the scene of the greatest American loss of life on D-Day – Omaha Beach. Unable to move off the beach, the soldiers edged their way forward with great difficulty and, by the end of that day, the total American dead and wounded totalled over three thousand.

After the war, the American Battle Monuments Commission developed a cemetery covering 172 acres of land donated by the French people. It eventually grew to include the graves of 9,387 American war dead of whom 307 are unknown. The headstones of white marble crosses and, when the soldier is Jewish, a Star of David, form an impressive geometric pattern that stands out against superbly maintained lawns. The memorial consists of a semi-circular colonnade with a loggia at each end with one showing details of the battle area engraved into the stone. As a tribute to young Americans who sacrificed their lives in Normandy, there is a 7-metre-high statue, the 'Spirit of American Youth'. At its base is the inscription: 'Mine eyes have seen the glory of the coming of the Lord.' In a semi-circular garden are the Walls of the Missing that lists the names of 1,557 missing American servicemen and rosettes mark the names of those later recovered and identified. At the side of the central pathway is a chapel with a mosaic ceiling depicting America blessing her sons as they depart to fight for freedom by land, sea and air. At the far western end of the cemetery there are two granite figures sculpted by Donald de Lue representing the United States and France and, at the edge of the cemetery where it overlooks Omaha Beach, there is a parapet with an orientation table indicating the various landing beaches. Amongst those buried in the cemetery are the sons of the former United States President Teddy Roosevelt, Brigadier Theodore Roosevelt, junior, who died on 12 June 1944 and his brother, Quentin Roosevelt, who lost his life in the First World War. Over the years, the families of many American servicemen have requested the repatriation of their dead and the bodies of some 14,000 men have been returned home.

The beach at St Laurent-sur-Mer today with its array of memorials dedicated to American servicemen.

A section of the American War Cemetery.

The American War Cemetery seen from the memorial.

Sons of former US President Teddy Roosevelt (*right and below*). Brigadier General Theodore Roosevelt, junior who led the 4th Infantry Division and died in 1944 following a heart attack after landing at Utah Beach.

Quentin Roosevelt who was killed in aerial combat in July 1918. Later his body was exhumed to be buried next to his brother in the American Military Cemetery.

US President Barack Obama accompanied by Prince Charles, British Prime Minister Gordon Brown, Canadian Prime Minister Stephen Harper and French President Nicholas Sarkozy celebrating the 65th anniversary of D-Day at the American Military Cemetery in 2009.

Ste Marie du Mont

The village of Sainte Marie du Mont lies a short distance from Utah Beach and, on D-Day, it was just within the area covered by the American 101st Airborne Division commanded by Major-General Maxwell Taylor. The 506th Parachute Infantry Regiment landed close to the village and since the village lay immediately behind one of the few remaining causeways across the flooded area behind the beach, it was of considerable strategic importance. The village itself was garrisoned by German troops and many of them were billeted in the homes of French families. The arrival of American paratroopers, some of whom landed in the centre of the town, led to fighting in the streets around the square and the church, which contained a German observation post, changed hands several times. During the morning, with the arrival of other American units, the German resistance was quickly overcome.

The village suffered relatively little damage and is much the same today as it was on D-Day. Of particular use to visitors are the fourteen notices dotted on the walls of the village that explain exactly what happened in the struggle to liberate the village.

Local people welcome American soldiers to Ste Marie du Mont.

The church tower was once used by the Germans as an observation post.

6 JUIN 1944

Au petit matin, le bourrelier assista derrière ses volets à un duel digne d'un western. Un para américain était sous ses fenêtres (maison au volets blancs) quand un allemand arriva, masqué par le monument aux morts. Ils se virent au dernier moment et tirèrent en même temps. Le parachutiste s'écroula, tué net. Il portait des gants de pécari. L'allemand grièvement blessé fut porté chez le boucher, où un médecin américain parvint à le sauver.

In the early morning, the harness maker, hidden behind his shutters, witnessed a duel worthy of any Western. An American paratrooper was crouched below his windows (the house with the white shutters) when a German soldier arrived, hidden behind the First World War Memorial. They saw each other at the same moment and fired at the same time. Shot dead, the paratrooper fell to the ground. He was wearing pigskin gloves. The seriously wounded German was carried to the butcher's shop where an American doctor managed to save his life.

5

One of the fourteen notices on the walls of the town that inform tourists of what exactly happened there on D-Day.

A museum in a town that remains very much committed to the years of occupation and liberation.

Ste Mère-Église

Midway between Carentan and Montebourg, the town of Ste Mère-Église is one of the most frequently visited by veterans and tourists to the Normandy battlefields. Originally the quiet town was the centre of a livestock breeding area but at 1.30 a.m. on the morning of D-Day the first American paratroopers of the US 82nd and 101st Airborne Divisions began to descend in and around the town. Commanded by Major-General Matthew Ridgway, the aim of the 82nd Division was to take the town and hold the bridges over the Rivers Douve and Merderet, whilst the purpose of 101st Division, led by Major-General Maxwell Taylor, was to secure the high ground and remaining road exits across the flooded area behind Utah Beach.

Unfortunately things did not entirely go to plan since many paratroopers landed far from their designated dropping areas and some in the areas flooded by the Germans when they opened the sluice gates immediately behind Utah Beach. The result was that many paratroopers and glider-borne soldiers perished in the water-logged area but this did not prevent the Americans from moving away from Utah Beach and joining up with those who had made the airborne drop. The men were often easy targets as they descended in the night sky and some gliders crashed on landing and, once on the ground, American soldiers used clicking devices to help them remain in contact with and provide identification for their comrades.

An American soldier takes a rest close to Ste Mère-Église.

American troops are welcomed into the town by local citizens.

The memorial to the Alexandre Renaud, the mayor of Ste Mère-Église at the time the town was liberated.

The stained glass windows in the church at Ste Mère-Église.

The D-Day museum at Ste Mère-Église.

US losses were heavy with the 82nd Division losing two thirds of its men and the 101st Division only able to muster 1,000 of its original number. In spite of this, the 505th Parachute Infantry Regiment, which had landed in the town square, managed to raise an American flag outside the town hall by 6 a.m. in the morning. German counter-attacks followed but, with the aid of tanks that arrived from Utah Beach, these were repulsed and the town was firmly in American hands by the afternoon of 7 June. Private John Steele was particularly unfortunate when his parachute harness caught on a corner of the church steeple. All he could do was to feign death and he remained there for two hours as his comrades fought in the square below. Elsewhere, in order to allow the wounded Colonel Benjamin Vanderport to keep in contact with his men, he was pushed around in a wheelbarrow. The town's priest, Abbé Roulland, bravely rang the church bells to summon help as fires caused by Allied bombing began to engulf the houses whilst Alexandre Renaud, the mayor and a local chemist, organised local people into a chain to pass buckets of water, hand-to-hand from the only water pump available.

Today, Ste Mère-Église remains dedicated to the events of 6 June 1944. In the square, the roof of the church carries a model of paratrooper John Steele who was a regular visitor to the town until his death in 1969. Inside the twelfth-century church there are stained glass windows dedicated to the 82nd Airborne Division financed by American war veterans. On the edge of the square lies an impressive Airborne Museum which covers all aspects of the events in the town and locality on D-Day and includes a restored CG-4A Hadrian Glider and a Dakota aircraft. Outside the town hall is a marker stone 'Kilometre Zero'. These markers were introduced by the French government in 1946 to indicate the route taken by General Leclerc's Free French 2nd Division. American soldiers who lost their lives in and around Ste Mère-Église were first buried locally but four years later they were removed though the original sites are still marked by memorials. There were twenty-two civilian casualties and these are listed on a memorial behind the 'Kilometre Zero' marker stone.

Secqueville-en-Bessin

Secqueville-en-Bessin, a small village which on D-Day had a population of less than two hundred, lies close to Bretteville-l'Orgueilleuse. It has a splendid eleventh-century church with a fine three-storey tower and a tall, impressive spire. Canadian soldiers had little difficulty in liberating the village on 7 June 1944.

To the east lies Secqueville-en-Bessin War Cemetery. It is a small cemetery that contains the graves of 117 men killed during the advance on Caen early in July 1944. Ninety-eight of the men were British, eighteen German and one unknown.

The impressive eleventh-century church in Secqueville-en-Bessin.

Secqueville-en-Bessin War Cemetery.

Tilly-sur-Seulles

After occupying Bayeux on 7 June 1944, the British 50th Division advanced southwards towards Tilly-sur-Seulles. The town, which lay to the west of Caen, was to be stubbornly defended by the 12th SS Panzer Division, the Hitlerjugend, and the Panzer Lehr Division. On 11 June, men of the 6th Battalion Durham Light Infantry entered the town but the next day the British were forced back as Tilly-sur-Seulles became the scene of some of the most bitter fighting of the Normandy campaign. On 16 June, the 2nd Battalion of the Essex Regiment again entered the town and two days later Tilly-sur-Seulles was finally liberated.

Today, the town has a splendid war museum, the *Musée de la Bataille de Tilly-sur-Seulles*, which is located in a twelfth-century church, the *Chapelle Notre Dame du Val*.

Close to the centre of the town is the Tilly-sur-Seulles War Cemetery which contains those that were killed during the heavy fighting for the town prior to 18 June. The cemetery contains 1,222 burials including 986 British many of them then serving in the 2nd Devonshire Regiment and the King's Own Yorkshire Light Infantry, as well as two New Zealanders, an Australian, a Canadian and 232 Germans.

Amongst those buried in the cemetery are an eighteen-year-old private soldier, John Gethin, who served in the Gordon Highlanders and came from Rhurnscoe in Yorkshire, Lieutenant Lord Edward Fitzmaurice, son of the Marquess of Landsdowne, Major Anthony Earley-Wilmot MC, a former Cambridge University scholar from Leamington Spa, and Captain Keith Douglas, a former Oxford University scholar from Bexhill-on-Sea. Douglas is a recognised war poet and amongst his works is *Aristocrats – I think I am Becoming a God.*

> *The noble horse with courage in his eye,*
> *clean in the bone, looks up at a shellburst:*
> *away fly the images of the shires*
> *but he puts the pipe back in his mouth.*
> *Peter was unfortunately killed by an 88;*
> *it took his leg away, he died in the ambulance.*
> *I saw him crawling on the sand, he said*
> *It's most unfair, they've shot my foot off.*
> *How can I live among this gentle*
> *obsolescent breed of heroes, and not weep?*

The war museum in Tilly-sur-Seulles.

Tilly-sur-Seulles War Cemetery.

Troarn

Troarn lies to the east of Caen and inland from Pegasus Bridge. One of the most important tasks given to the British 6th Airborne Division was to destroy the bridges over the River Dives and so protect the Allied bridgehead from a possible German counter-attack. The most important bridge was close to Troarn and the plan was to send a Parachute Squadron of the Royal Engineers to destroy the bridge. At 4 a.m. on a small number of paratroopers assembled and, led by Major J. C. A. Roseveare, began their journey to the bridge.

Making only slow progress on foot, they commandeered a jeep and entered the centre of Troarn before, under heavy German fire, driving through the length of the village. They finally stopped by the River Dives and used explosives to blow up the bridge.

Roseveare thought it unwise to drive back through the village so they made their back on foot. The village of Troarn was finally liberated by 41st Royal Marine Commando on 17 August. For his 'bravery and conspicuous gallantry' the major was awarded the Distinguished Service Order.

Veterans and local people gather to commemorate the 68th anniversary of the daring destruction of the bridge.

Today, in the village square there is a plaque on the wall that commemorates the success of the men of the 3rd Parachute Squadron Royal Engineers and, close to the bridge over the River Dives, a memorial to Major Roseveare and his men. In the village's communal cemetery there are the graves of three British soldiers. All in their twenties, they are Private Henry Carter and Sergeants John Davies and John Lliffe who served with the 8th Battalion of the Parachute Regiment and died on 6 June 1944.

Valognes

Once a market town of broad streets and grand houses that earned it the name 'The Versailles of Normandy', during June 1944 American bombing reduced a large part of the town to rubble and very few of the splendid houses survived. Earlier, the town had been the headquarters of General von Schlieben but, after the fall of Montebourg on 19 June (see pages 115–116) he left the town to concentrate on the defence of Cherbourg. Subsequently, the US forces faced little resistance when they occupied the town.

Although today little remains of its architectural heritage, Valognes is once again a colourful and vibrant town and its citizens still retain memories of its glorious past. The town church which was badly damaged in 1944 has been totally rebuilt and the town has two museums devoted to the history of the manufacture of the apple-based drinks cider and calvados.

American troops witness the devastation of Valognes.

The ruins of the church in 1944.

The rebuilt church as it appears today.

Valognes today.

Ver-sur-Mer

Ver-sur-Mer lies on the eastern edge of Gold Beach. On 6 June 1944, the area was assigned to the British 50th Division and the first troops ashore at 7.25 a.m. were men from the 5th East Yorkshire Regiment and the 6th Green Howards. Since the coast rises gradually above the beach, there was little cover but once flail-tanks had been used to remove the mines, the British troops were able to move quickly off the beaches towards a known German battery at Mont Fleury.

It was here that CSM Stan Hollis showed great bravery and became the only man to be awarded the Victoria Cross on D-Day.

Stan Hollis was born in Redcar in Yorkshire in 1912. After attending a local school, he worked at his father's fish and chip shop until he became an apprentice at a Whitby shipping company. After a period of illness, he married and worked as a lorry driver. In 1939, Hollis enlisted in the Territorial Army and at the start of the Second World War he was sent to France with the 6th Battalion of the Green Howards. In 1940, he managed to be evacuated from Dunkirk. He then served in North Africa and Italy and during this time was promoted to corporal, sergeant and finally company sergeant-major. On 6 June, CSM Stan Hollis successfully led the storming of two pill-boxes and then rescued two of his men who had been left behind. For his bravery, he was awarded the Victoria Cross. Later in the year, he was wounded and returned to Britain and in October of that year was decorated by King George VI.

In spite of the fact that the people in Ver-sur-Mer had to endure a bombardment, when the British soldiers finally appeared in the streets they were welcomed by French civilians who cheered them and threw them flowers.

Today, close to the centre of the town there are memorials to the British troops who liberated Ver-sur-Mer and an upright anchor mounted on a stone base and inscribed: '*Hommage et reconnaissance a nos liberateurs.*' The memorial was donated by Julien Costy, a local fisherman.

The remains of the German battery at Mont Fleury today.

British troops of the Northumbrian Division passing through Ver-sur-Mer.

CSM Stan Hollis.

Vierville-sur-Mer

On 6 June 1944, Vierville-sur-Mer lay at the western end of Omaha Beach. The bombing and bombardment of the German defensive positions appeared to have had little effect as, along this stretch of coast, the American 1st and 29th Infantry Divisions coming ashore were mown down and suffered heavy casualties. It was not until mid-morning that the 5th Rangers managed to breach the German defences and establish a means of exit from the beach. Today, much remains to remind visitors of that day.

On the seafront amongst a great many memorials and monuments and there is a *Comité du Débarquement* and close to the remains of a German bunker, a section of a Mulberry Harbour that, unlike the similar harbour at Arromanches (see pages 15–18), failed to survive a storm. On a platform there is a monument to the men of the National Guard who fought valiantly on the beaches and nearby, on a grassed area, there are monuments to the 29th United States Infantry Division and a plaque to the 5th Ranger Battalion.

Some distance away is the Château de Vierville that served as the headquarters of the US 11th Port Regiment Army from 8 June until 21 July.

American soldiers begin to struggle ashore near Vierville-sur-Mer.

The remains of a German bunker and a section of the destroyed Mulberry harbour close to the beach at Vierville-sur-Mer.

The *Comité du Débarquement* monument.

Memorial to the National Guard at Vierville-sur-Mer.

The Château de Vierville.

The beach at Vierville-sur-Mer today.

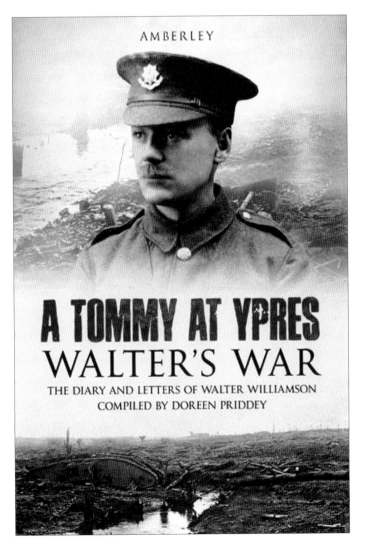

A Tommy at Ypres
Walter's War
Walter Williamson

In this remarkable diary we travel with Walter Williamson from
Birkenhead to France and onward to the Ypres Salient, where his vivid
recollections describe his part in the 188th Brigade's involvement in
the Battle of St Julien at the opening of the Third Battle of Ypres.

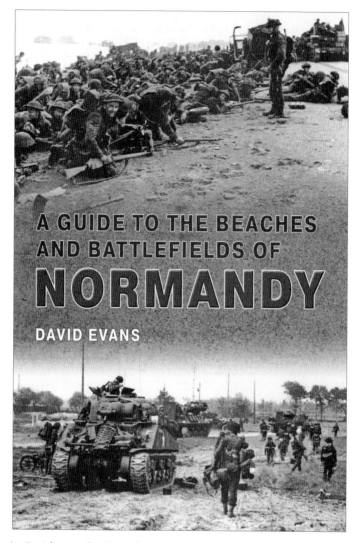

A Guide to the Beaches and Battlefields of Normandy

David Evans

Accompanied by photographs, maps and drawings, this guide
provides an accessible background to the momentous events of
6 June, as well as a complete guide to each and every town, village,
beach, battery and cemetery that figured in the battle.

978 1 84868 184 2
176 pages

Available from all good bookshops or order direct
from our website www.amberleybooks.com